THE MOON IS LIKE A
SILVER SICKLE

ALSO EDITED AND TRANSLATED BY MIRIAM MORTON

From Two to Five, by Kornei Chukovsky

A Harvest of Russian Children's Literature

Fierce and Gentle Warriors, stories by Mikhail Sholokhov

Twenty-two Russian Tales for Young Children by Leo Tolstoy

Shadows and Light, nine stories by Anton Chekhov

The First Song, by Semyon Rosenfeld

The House of the Four Winds, by Colette Vivier

Voices from France, ten stories by French Winners of the Nobel Prize
   for Literature

Fifteen by Maupassant

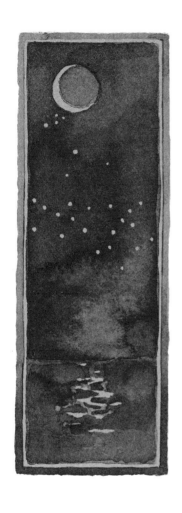

THE
MOON
IS LIKE A
SILVER
SICKLE

A Celebration of Poetry
by Russian Children

Collected and Translated by

MIRIAM MORTON ₑd

Illustrated by

EROS KEITH

Simon and Schuster   New York

Published by Simon and Schuster, Children's Book Division
Rockefeller Center, 630 Fifth Avenue
New York, New York 10020
First Printing
SBN 671-65198-6
Library of Congress Catalog Card Number: 72-77768
Manufactured in the United States of America
Designed by Jack Jaget

Dedicated to the memory of
RUTH HILL VIGUERS

TRANSLATOR'S NOTE

More often than not Russian children who write poetry with a degree of seriousness come under the literary influence of men and women (teachers and leaders of poetry circles) who think it wrong to insist that the fledgling poets strictly follow metrical patterns or other standard norms of prosody. They have observed that the young poet "freezes" under such constraints. And the aim, they hold, is not to shackle him but to give him wings. . . . With this in mind, the translator consciously avoided rendering the Russian poem into English with greater regularity of rhyme and rhythm or felicity of cadence than the child's version had.

The translator's primary concern was to preserve the child's vision and to capture its beauty of expression. The extent of adaptation was dictated mainly by the consideration: how would the child have written his poem were English his native language?

M.M.

CONTENTS

INTRODUCTION

The Moon Is Like a Silver Sickle is a selection of ninety-two poems written by Russian children—a few as young as seven or eight and some in their early teens. The book also includes a number of verses composed by preschoolers. Most of the poems were created within the last five or six years.

The young Soviet poets represented in this volume live in some thirty different cities, towns and villages scattered throughout their immense country—in places ranging from the European borders of the USSR all the way across to a small town at the other end of the country on the island of Sakhalin, in the Pacific Ocean.

Forty-six of the poems were written by boys and forty-six by girls.*

The selections were made on the basis of merit alone, but an important consideration for inclusion was whether it was possible to translate the lines into English without loss of subtlety of meaning or the beauty of image and expression.

The writing of these young Russian poets has the essence of fine poetry. Their lines often speak of moods, feelings and thoughts in a personal, subjective way, as does good adult poetry. By means of heightened language and in tones of sensitivity, they delight, move, or excite the reader with the special forcefulness of the language of poetry.

---

*In Russian a boy's name usually ends with a consonant (Ivan, Alexander, Mikhail) and a girl's name *always* ends with a vowel (Nina, Natasha). In this book, the exceptions—boys' names which end with a vowel—are Alesha, Anatoli, Andrei, Borya, Ilya, Kolya, Kostya, Nikita, Sasha, Sergei, Seriozha, Volodya and Yuri.

These poems from Russia are unique because they reflect the life style, ideas and ideals of a nation quite different from our own. They give us insights into a country that is still largely a mystery to us. Yet there are many verses here which prove once again that experiences and aspirations of boys and girls are similar the world over. With keen eyes and sincere hearts the young Soviet poets in this volume sought to write down their observations of themselves, of their immediate world and of the world at large.

The treasury of Russian poetry, though vast and varied, is written almost entirely in rhyme. Contemporary poets generally follow this long tradition, for it is held by Russian men of letters (as well as by many in other countries) that rhyming renders a poem more musical; that it enhances meaning and the poem stays longer in the reader's memory; that it helps the poet have better control of his theme; and that the quest for a rhyming word often takes the poet to byways of spontaneous and original association which give greater lyricism or force to his expression.

Most of the young poets in this collection, too, have written in rhyme, although some experimented with freer forms. The translator has tried, as far as possible, to follow the preference of the young author in this regard. Unfortunately, English has far fewer rhyming words than Russian does. At times, therefore, she found it necessary to sacrifice some rhyming for the sake of preserving the poet's meaning and the beauty of his utterance.

With this much said, let us now allow the poems to speak for themselves, and for the boys and girls who wrote them.

The verses on the title pages for the separate sections are from poems by classical and modern Russian poets.

M.M.

DISCOVERIES AND DELIGHTS

A magic landscape,
My heart's delight,
A full moon's brightness,
A plain sheer white.

AFANASY FET

THE FLOWER

It blossomed.
The fly buzzes about
In admiration.
Even the cat—
Even he
Comes,
Smells it
With approbation.

VOLODYA LAPIN
Age 9

THE BLACK PANTHER

Like night in broad daylight
She lies staring at me.
Her eyes burn in the darkness,
The darkness that—is she.

KOSTYA RAIKIN
Age 11

SPRING MOOD

I'm bursting with impatience!
The stream warbles in the wood,
First leaves strum in the treetops,
Spring music has set the mood.

I'm bursting with impatience!
I've waited for spring too long!
The birds are back, the birds are singing,
I'll explode if I don't burst into song!

VOLODYA LAPIN
Age 13

A pretty boat
Sails on the sea,
Sails on the sea.
Behind the boat
A herring is afloat
In the sea,
In the sea.

NIKITA TOLSTOY
Age 4

STORM AT SEA

Let it rock!
Let it roll!
Under the stern,
Waters
Rumble and churn!
Merge with the clouds,
Waves of the sea!
Rise higher! Rise higher!
So that the mast pierces the sky,
So that my heart . . . beats high.

ALEXANDER KOTUL'SKY
Age 12

THE YOUNG COSSACK

Bushy forelock,
Sheepskin cape,
Saber of gold,
Eighteen years old.

ANDREI KAMENSKY
Age 10

Open, open the gates—
The sun is coming up in
the sky!

TATYA

Age 3

OUT SKIING

Winter goes on, winter goes on,
Still spreading its hushed whiteness,
Still waving, still waving its wand,
Still dressing the birch in queen's likeness.
The day's last ray blinds with its glacial gleam,
While there, in the shade, the snow is blue-blue
Like a lingering phantom in a long, long dream.
I rush downhill on my skittery skis,
I feel the rush of the days toward spring.
Impatient, impatient am I for the New!
Wind! Catch me as I fly, as I sing.
In this wintry silence already I hear
The tinkle, the trickle of spring.

LARISSA SHAKHOVICH

Age 11

MY BICYCLE AND ME

I have a brand-new bicycle.
I ride it day and night.
The cock and hens and ducks
All run from us in fright.

LORA KULICHKOVA
Age 8

A BIT OF COBWEB

The day frolics through the village,
Laughing, playing pranks.
A cobweb on a twig—
Like a bit of lace it hangs.

LENA SARCHUK
Age 12

The radish is blooming,
The drum is booming,
And I drink tea—
Excessively.

IRINA
Age 5

EREVAN IS MY CITY

Erevan, my city Erevan!
Fountains, how you splash and splash!
My face in your coolness I dip,
Take a drink, and off I dash.

MAYA NIKOGOSIAN
Age 5

IN AUTUMN

The gaunt pines sigh,
Steady themselves against the sky,
Counting their past springs.
As more cheerful memories they search,
Nearby, swaying carefree in the wind,
Like a slender girl, is a slender birch.

TANYA DINSBURG
Age 14

THE SORCERESS

Winter! Oh, Sorceress! Queen!
The earth you dress in perfection.
In the mirror of your ice,
The Moon admires its reflection.

Into a fairyland you transform the woods.
Gifts of fine raiment you bestow on trees.
You endow the world with splendor,
With a Good Fairy's magical ease.

LIUDA PAZHARSKAYA
Age 12

THE PUMPKIN

It lies ripe in the turnip patch,
Looking as if it is about
To wave its little tail
And with pleasure grunt out loud.

SERGEI ORLOV
Age 8

A CELEBRATION

With songs and dances—a celebration,
They greet us merrily at the station.
Fellow passengers call to me:
"Find out the name of the village—go and see."
"Harvest!" I hear myself saying,
"They're celebrating the end of the haying!"
We'd join them but we have far to go,
And the whistle is about to blow.
With songs and dances—a celebration,
They bid us farewell at the station.

VOLODIMIR SHEPELEV

Age 12

I look out of my window
And see a clear day,
A bit of bright leafiness,
A sail's shadow on the bay.

OLYA

Age 6

My teddy stands in the nook,
Smiling at a little book.
He is ashamed, indeed,
That he knows not how to read.

OLGA

Age 4

The blue wings
    in the white frost
    in the white frost
    silvery.

The plane glides,
    into the clouds it dives,
    into the clouds it dives
    the plane.

And with skill
    to the stars he soars,
    to the stars he soars
    our pilot.

ANDREI KARLOV

Age 7

THE BROOK

All dappled with sunshine,
On ripples the brook.
In the palm of its hand
All of spring it took.
It reflects the young willow
Gaily dipping her hair,
As two curious snowdrops
Lean over and stare.

LIUDA ALAVERDOSHVILI
Age 13

BEFORE THE SUMMER DOWNPOUR

The wind tugs at my two pigtails,
Hurries on to add to the mower's bustle.
The clouds pile up, darken the sun.
Huge raindrops make the leaves rustle.

SVETA KOLOSOVA
Age 11

THE SIZE OF HIM!

He stands there
At the curb,
In his long Red Army coat
He's superb!
A splendid sight—
His amazing height!
Ten feet tall,
Windburned, slim—
People exclaim:
"Look at him!"
Their wonder
They can't conceal:
Someone murmurs,
"Is he real?!"

ALEXANDER KOTUL'SKY
Age 10

THE PATH ON THE SEA

The moon this night is like a silver sickle
Mowing a field of stars.
It has spread a golden runner
Over the rippling waves.
With its winking shimmer
This magic carpet lures me
To fly to the moon on it.

INNA MULLER
Age 13

THE WATERMELON

I've bought me a watermelon.
It's quite a heavy load!
It's striped like a zebra,
Green and fat as a toad.

I'm carrying it home,
Can't wait to put it down!
It's quite a heavy load,
This delicious, juicy toad.

LIUDA ALAVERDOSHVILI
Age 12

RUSSIAN SNOW

Snow . . . it isn't simply white,
Snow . . . it can be gentle or bite,
It can be beckoning, brazen, or insolent,
Sunny . . . or obstinately inclement.

Dismal like a mournful shroud,
Or joyous and crunchingly loud.
Velvety, fluffy, embracing,
Or skiing snow, hard and bracing.

Moonlit, boundless, deep,
Blanketing the steppe, deep in sleep,
Missing old times—sleighbells ringing,
Coachmen's calls and merrymakers' singing.

OLGA TEITELMAN
Age 12

THANK YOU

Thank you, Sun, for being here!
Thank you, Stream, for being near!
Thank you, Flowers!
Thank you, Summer Showers!

LILY BREEK
Age 6

LIKE A SPARKLING BEAD

The day is full of mischief, it winks,
Scowls, laughs in my face.
The girl—sparkling like a bead in the sun—
Walks past me with tantalizing grace.

How translucent you are!
Like pure water. No, more rare!
With your luminous gaiety,
Where are you rolling, oh, where?

What color are you really—
Little dewdrop, little bride?
You don't look like the others—
The ones I have tried . . .

A chance passerby in midsummer:
Now you are gone, but here I stand
With you in my mind
Like a sparkling bead in the hand.

ILYA BEDNIAKOV
Age 15

OUR CAT

Though it is New Year's Eve,
Vasili's mood is bad.
He's not asked to the party—
So Vasili is very mad.

VOLODYA LAPIN
Age 11

A SENSE
OF
SELF

I want to find the essence of
All things, each part:
In word, in groping for a way,
In turmoiled heart.

BORIS PASTERNAK

I want time to run, to race for me,
With the haste of the fleetest ski.
Shorter my life may then be,
But so much, so much will I see.

VOLODYA LAPIN

Age 13

The weather is gloomy!
The grown-ups are gloomy.
I alone am busy being gay!
They look at me gloomily,
But I smile at them and say:
Tri-lea, tri-lea, tri-lay!

ANA TARASOVA

Age 6

To fling songs into the air,
            laugh
                    and shout!
To trip,
        rise,
                and run from doubt.
To smile at passing mankind,
And wait:
                search,
                        hope,
                                find!
In every way to find
                and not compromise,
In every way to go on
                and not temporize.
To trust the wind,
            the stars,
                    and eyes . . .

YURI GRIZLOV
Age 14

Our garden . . . is my world.
Mine, the hills, the seas,
    forests and fields.
Mine is the whole world!
To chase! To skip!
To roam! To loll!
To soar like a dove!
To dance! To love!

NINA GLEKIVA
Age 6

I might repeat in every line
What others have already said,
But how I think and what I feel
Is what I have achieved, and
Is wholly mine.

SASHA ALEKSANDROVSKY
Age 14

SOMEONE I KNOW . . .

People pass me in the street.
What they think?—I couldn't care less.
In me something is stirring:
What?—dare I, dare I guess!
The whole of me is suffused with a glow
As I wander in search of my spring,
As in the mist and stillness I wonder:
March—what will it bring?
Without the answer I return home at dawn,
Hang my soul on a nail, or some such thing.
I hear a whisper: "Forget it,
There is in this life no real spring."
In my sleep someone steps on my soul,
Points an accusing finger of blame . . .
Next day in the recklessness of noon
I crave for my spring just the same.

ANONYMOUS (girl)
Age 13

CHOICE

Could be, they were broken,
maybe they were hidden,
but lost are the bars,
down are the barriers,
gone are the locks
irretrievably.
Now you go wherever you wish.
Now you are no longer fettered.
You feel joy,
you feel alarm.
You can go wherever you wish—
to the end of the earth or the nearest mound—
as you wish.
To the fence—if you are a cock,
to the water—if a loon bird,
to the eaves—if a pigeon,
to the stars—if a Gagarin.*

RITA MAL'KOVA
Age 15

* Yuri Gagarin was the first man to orbit the earth.

THE NONCONFORMIST

Once more the rising sun has lit a
  streak of fire in the sky.
But in the morning of the new day,
Into the hastening trolley bus
I am pushed like a cork into a bottle.
Man loves the dawn for its freshness, I think,
For its promise of new beginnings.
In the morning, therefore, I'm not frightened
That I have chosen to lead a life
  unlike that of other young men.

ANATOLI IVANUSHKIN
Age 15

To infinite heights will the roads of life
Spiral me according to my own taste.
I won't listen to those who forever repeat:
"Slow down—haste makes waste."

VOLODYA LAPIN
Age 14

WE, THE YOUNG

With all sorts of things we are crammed.
Everywhere we are praised and we are damned.
In us there's so much of the superficial,
In us there's so much that's superfluous,
In us there's so much that is shallow,
In us there's so much that is spiteful,
In us there's so much that is good . . .
But people turn on us with distrust.
They are adult and . . . they are dull.
In us all is unpredictable, matinal,
All is in outgoing and incoming tides.
Spring waters are muddied, troubled
So that they may be clear by fall . . .

MIKHAIL GURVICH
Age 15

THE TIME HAS COME . . .

Mother,
> the time has come:
>> you can hear

The train's urgent signal,
Its stern call for departure.
I am on my way:
> I see with
>> great wonder

How soon in the mist you have vanished—
Like the March snow in the field over yonder,
Like the first ray of morning
When the sun moves into the clouds.
This must be
> this must be
>> this must be.

What if tears sting my eyes—
Your trust will be my reward,
Make me proud
Give me strength
Sustain me in life's battles.
I hear the roll of the drums:
It is time to face the world on my own.
Let the harsh winds strike—
That sooner will my back be stiffened.
Farewell!
Till we meet
> till we meet
>> till we meet!

SERGEI VORONOV

Age 15

FAMILY
AND
FRIENDS

The dawn breaks over the mooring.
I'm homing.
In memory all from the outset I trace.
The land moves closer, bringing old friends.

MIKHAIL LUKONIN

TWO MOTHERS

I love my house,
I love our little stream,
I love its long shore,
And the pretty birch tree
Growing at our door.
To name all this—I'd name it
My birthplace! My homeland.
Over it is the same blue dome of sky
As over my entire Motherland, which is
Always with me, for me—everywhere.
Oh, Mama, you who sang me cradlesongs—
Don't mind that I call you both, "Mother."
You are the first, my country—the second.
I'll ever sing praises to my two mothers.

IRA SHEYANOVA
Age 10

MY MOTHER AND ME

My mother and me—
We scream and we battle.
Her brain's made of straw,
Her heart, of scrap metal!

ANONYMOUS (boy)
Age 6

TO A FRIEND

I like
       others—
              for their modesty,
I like
       some—
              for their dignity,
              for their humor,
                     restless vitality.

And you, for what!
When I am miserable,
        I pass the modest ones,
When I am miserable
        I pass the dignified,
        all the humorous,
               those with restless vitality.
I come to you,
        that says all.

VITALY SHLENSKY
Age 15

AT HOME

Saturday, Saturday,
A day welcome and gay.
We shop, sweep, dust, and scrub,
(But despite the chores,)
I love Saturday and its hubbub.

ANONYMOUS (boy)
Age 12

Three little birches—
Three little sisters
All in a row.
I hug them,
I kiss them,
Then like a Mama
I go.

MAYA NIKOGOSIAN
Age 6

ALONE

The leaves shudder, the branch shakes,
Into the clearing steps the elk.
He is alone—he has strayed from the herd:
Not because he's old or feeble—
Men had come, rounded up the others,
Driven them far, far from their forest home.
And here he is—still free.
But he feels no joy.
He is all alone.

KOSTYA RAIKIN
Age 8

A hungry wolf is in the street,
He spies three chicks—a treat!
He's jumping over the fence!
Run friends! Away you go!
Beware, here comes your foe!

IRINA
Age 4

THE REFRIGERATOR

It is good
to be alive—
with our 'fridge
to thrive.
We don't worry
about the cream,
everything is cold
when tasted,
Nothing now
spoils,
nothing
will be wasted!

ALLA GENIKOVA

Age 9

Hi there, friend or foe,
Hi there, mosquito.
Where have you been?
"To the little store."
What brought you there?
"A small cloud of snow."
Where is it now?
"I ate it long ago."

IRINA IVANOVA

Age 4

MAKING FRIENDS

Once at midday, at the zoo,
I saw not one elephant but two.
They gazed at me, asked to know:
Are you Volodya, yes or no?
The baby looked just one year old,
His tiny trunk I longed to hold.
He offered it, trembling with joy
To be making friends with so big a boy.

VOLODYA LAPIN
Age 12

Grandma snores
When she sleeps.
From under her pillow
A baby whale creeps,
And I hear it peep:
"Grandma snores,
That means she's asleep."

NIKITA TOLSTOY
Age 4

MY HAMMER

I bang, bang, bang,
Whack, whack, whack,
Pound in the nail and the tack.
I make a stool,
I shoe my horse,
A wobbly bench I reinforce.
We're the best of friends—
My hammer and my hands.

ALESHA
Age 10

THE TEAKETTLE

It whistles, hisses, burbles and boils.
We snatch it off the fire.
Our guests and us it fills to the gills,
With all the sweet tea we desire.

VOLODYA LAPIN
Age 10

THE BABY TIGERS

The early morning sunbeam
Sought out the waking wee tigers.
There they were, in the grass,
Small and fluffy as kittens.
Their empty tummies rumbled,
They grumbled and they yawned,
Opening wide their red mouths.
Now came the tigress from the hunt—
Huge, fierce and fearsome.
For their meal she had killed a doe.
And deep in the forest, beneath a tree,
The doe's infant deer lie crying.

KOSTYA RAIKIN
Age 11

NONSENSE

My little brother Vovka's head
With nonsense verse is full:
Everything is topsy-turvy
In the rhymes he learns at school.

The Moon shines in the daytime,
The Sun blazes through the night.
A Turtle with a whip in hand,
Rides a horse with all its might.

The Dog meows,
The Cat howls,
The Rabbit grunts,
The Duck growls.

And Mousie says to Elephant,
"Come to my hole you must!"
There the twosome gnaw away
At a little tiny crust.

If other rhyming nonsense
Were topsy-turvied in certain ways,
Would on Vovka's next report card
Show, not D's and F's but only A's?

NASTYA KORALOVA
Age 12

A RIDDLE

She glows brighter than the sun.
She is busier than the sea.
She is dearer than the most precious stone.

She is my mother.

MAYA NIKOGOSIAN
Age 6

THE OCTOBER ANNIVERSARY

The city gleams in crimson red.
The festive mood throughout has spread.
In a sunny room, this holiday
Sit Petya and his friend Andrei.
On the wall, draped in crimson red,
Hangs Grandfather's picture—a man who bled
And fought for freedom—won it hard,
Gave it to the people, for them to guard.

SERIOZHA SLEZSKY
Age 11

LOSING FRIENDS

I keep losing friends.
Without quarrels. Without rancor.
I am strewn with splinters of
                    broken friendships.
Yet I remember: some were so good
They didn't need to grow wings!
But I keep losing friends.
"Don't abandon me, stay!"
I want to cry out,
And again touch soul to soul,
And again believe them the best
                    in the world,
And that all will be as before!
Silence fills my room—not even
                    an echo responds.
My wary eye looks at me quizzically.

ASYA GUTKINA
Age 14

LOVING

Half a moon
sheds half a light,
half a love,
                    no light at all.

ROBERT ROZHDESTVENSKY

A caressing breeze touched
The green glistening leaves,
I touched her hand
At parting . . .

ANONYMOUS* (boy)
Age 13

My mama has been clever,
She hasn't spanked me ever!
Oh, Mama, my Mama
Always love, love, love me!
My love for you I'll now double
And never give you any trouble.

ANYA
Age 6

* A winning poem in a love-poetry contest for secondary school students.

I LOVE . . .

I love the gentle dewdrop
On the lacy leaf of birch,
The melting icicle in my palm,
And the cool sand in the brook.

I love the cornflower in the meadow—
Blue as a bit of azure sky,
The strong, fragrant smell of hot bread,
The rippling streamlet of rain water.

I love the snow-white smoke of fog,
The glow and red flush of dawn,
The fleecy caravans of clouds . . .
How much in the world I love!

TANYA MITROFANOVA
Age 13

AN OFFERING OF JOY

Where willows bend like rainbows,
Where peace and beauty toy,
I'll draw from the vernal spring
A pailful of clear joy.

    The sun will shimmer on the surface,
    A stray petal may alight on top,
    I'll walk slowly up the path,
    So as not to spill a single drop.

I'll take it home and keep it cool
For a wanderer weary of solitude.
I'll offer him a taste of rainbow,
A gift of the forest's quietude.

    I'll make this my life's work:
    To others I'll often bring
    Joy from a vernal spring.

SVETLANA EREMINA
Age 14

LENIN

I know
Where your wound hurts,
Which
None of the statues show.
In the squares
You stand ever
Lifelike,
Bareheaded, unsheltered,
Your broad palm
Raised against all winds.
I've come, my friend,
To button your coat.

YURA ARTIUSCHANKO
Age 12

TO LENINGRAD

To me Leningrad appears
     dove-blue and tender.
A gentle blue are its rains,
               its nights,
                    its River Neva.
The slender girls, too,
           are a soft sky-blue,
As though the Neva anointed them.
In Leningrad my dark eyes shine blue—
It is a miracle! What is its source?
Is it the kindness,
The openhearted goodness of this city,
The color of doves . . .

NATASHA BUGAKOVA
Age 14

A wondrous city is Moscow!
An ancient city is Moscow!
What a Kremlin has Moscow!
What towers in Moscow!
There are Frenchmen in Moscow!
There are Chinese in Moscow!
And everyone praises the city of Moscow!

TANIUSHA
Age 6

THE LITTLE GIRL

A fragile, crystalline figurine,
Clear as the heavens her eyes, and pale.
There is something of the Snow Maiden in her—
As if she would defy blizzard and gale.

Over her head the downy clouds float,
As fast as swift birds fly.
Like a slender shoot she stands,
Stretching, growing toward the sky.

TANYA IADCHENKO
Age 12

The sun is today so enchanting,
In the silken blue of the heavens,
That every petal in every daisy
Is this day in love with it.

INNA MULLER
Age 13

GOOD MORNING!

Good morning bright morning!
Sunshine of purest gold!
Come wind, come
Our banner unfold!
Now we'll sing in honor of
Our Motherland-the-Fair!
Fly song, fly
Clear across my land!

TANYA NICHIPORUM
Age 11

WAR
AND
PEACE

Do the Russians want war?
Ask the silence that bears and bore
Over our endless field and plain
The deafening answer of our slain.

YEVGENY YEVTUSHENKO

SOMETHING PEACEFUL

Asking his sister for paper and pencil,
The child sat down at the table to draw.
"What is
              our man doing?"
The mother asked her busy son.
"Look, I drew a battle—
My bomber,
              it blew up this tank . . ."
The soldier's widow shook her head:
"Why draw war, my boy?"
                          she said.
He turned over the paper,
                          heaved a sigh,
And this time drew a field of rye.
"The Harvest"—his title—
                          now dived from the sky.
Said the widow,
              brushing away a tear:
"What a lovely scene you have here!"

TANYA TSYGANOK

Age 14

The house is in ruins,
Its roof on the ground.
The children play soldiers
Inside and around.

IRINA IVANOVA
Age 6

I may not know them all by name,
Yet they are my closest kin—
For am I not alive today
Because they died for me.

ANONYMOUS* (boy)
Age 13

* Schoolmate of high school boys who were killed defending Moscow, in W.W.II. The poem is inscribed on a monument to these young patriots.

THE CHILDREN OF VIETNAM

The children of Vietnam dream of bombings.
The children of Vietnam dream of blood and
                death.
They see the world no longer with children's
                eyes.
Daytime but prolongs the terror of their
                nights.

This we never forget!
We remember the courage of our fathers,
And the meaning becomes ever clearer
Of the call: "Be prepared!"

Our school lessons end
With the welcome ringing of the bell.
Their lessons stop with the burst of
                bombs.
A sound so terrifying but so familiar.

Our Vietnamese friends, we do not forget!
We remember the courage of our forebears,
We are resolved, we affirm,
Take the vow: "Always prepared!"

OLGA TEITELMAN
Age 12

THE LAST SOLDIER

Who will you be—last soldier to perish?
A Russian, a Greek, a Zulu, or a German?
The calendar may not mark the date of your death,
But one thing'll be known, that you were human.

People may forget you, soldier,
Though a neighbor may recall a bit of your past—
How as a kid you chased a ball in his yard—
Not knowing that you would be the last . . .

You will never return to life,
The years of your youth to cherish.
Weep, o mankind, and laugh! This man
Was the last soldier to perish.

SERGEI MOROZOV
Age 15

BORDERS

The boy sat listening closely.
He was thinking hard about his world.
The children with crayons in their hands,
Were tracing (on maps) unfamiliar lands.

I talked to them about our globe,
Pointing to the least-known states.
The boy spoke up wanting to know:
Which was his nation's friend, which a foe.

"There are both kinds," was my glib reply.
The class resumed the tracing.
"Why doesn't the world get rid of all
    borders?" he said.
His young voice trembled, he bowed his head.

How was I to explain to this child,
(Since his young voice trembled . . .),
How answer the sore question he had raised?!
Since first between men's souls
    the borders must be erased.

SVETA MOSOVA
Age 15

THOUGHTS
AND
HOPES

I am in the all, the all in me . . .

FYODOR TIUTCHEV

I saw an apple
In the royal garden.
I did not envy it—
It was behind bars,
Behind bars . . .

BORYA
Age 9

THE LITTLE HOUSE

It stands there under the open skies,
Taking lashings from the rain,
Taking beatings from the hail,
But it does not complain.

ALESHA
Age 9

If only I were able
To speak like beast and bird,
Then listening to the sparrow,
I'd know what I've heard.

I'd know what the frog
So loudly croaks in the creek,
And what, when all is quiet at night,
The mice say as they squeak.

I'd know what the chickadee sings,
And why the finch sets up a twitter,
Why it is that the owl can't sleep,
Or what the cat purrs to her litter.

I'd know why in the wood so still,
So loudly weeps the whippoorwill.

BORYA LAPIN
Age 12

In America there is mourning.
In America there is shame.
Kennedy lies killed
Before the whole world.

ANDREI KARLOV
Age 9

A WEEK AFTER THE FIRST SPUTNIK

Fellows, is there anyone among you
Who does not yearn
To fly to the Moon
And to return?

It was all to happen,
I give you my word:
A place in the spaceship
For me was reserved.

But Sputnik would not fly
Without a mutt!
It would have been futile
For me to rebut.

So, though it caused me
Infinite pain,
The dog was to fly,
The man to remain!

ANONYMOUS (boy)

Age 12

THE LIONESS AND HER CUB

The baby lion had strayed, was lost,
When the pride went to the water.
The lioness mourned, for every mother
      needs a child,
Even if it is a naughty son or daughter.

VOLODYA LAPIN
Age 12

THE WILD FLOWER AND THE ROSE

A wild flower once sought the friendship
      of a rose.
Its disdainful response made the wild flower's
      heart ache.
How many parents claim superiority for their young?
And how many children such parents forsake!

DAVID NIKOGOSIAN
Age 12

No matter how he ties
His knot of vicious lies,
Truth, defying all,
Will hack it
Like an ax.

SASHA ALEKSANDROVSKY
Age 14

THE RADIANCE OF CREATIVITY

May he be scientist or bard,
No need for differentiation:
Each is—radiance from the self-same star,
Its vital, vibrant continuation . . .

OLYA BESHENKOVSKAYA
Age 15

In a poor old village
Lived a poor old man.
He was no longer strong—
He has lived too long.

LIDA
Age 5

A THOUGHT

Water poured into tumblers
Takes on their shapes.
Soft-bodied and captive,
Through the glass it gapes.

There are people as formless:
They nod to both right and wrong,
Pour themselves into another's mold,
So eager are they to get along.

They want to be agreeable.
They leave things as they are.
This is simpler—far less trouble
Than to condemn, jolt, or jar.

Well, what good will *they* achieve?
A stone, though to bits it be blown,
Unlike people behind self-imposed bars,
Has at least lived a life of its own.

Let it be sharp, since a stone it is.
Its blow harsh not painless.
I seek outspoken, fervent friends,
I shun the spineless.

SASHA UKACHEV
Age 15

THE QUESTION

Something follows everything:
Dawn follows night,
Sunset, the golden day,
Warmth, the cold,
Song, the silence,
Parting, the years together,
The ice of doubt, the fire of beginnings.
Is this much? Is this little?
There's no measure. I don't know.
Tens of centuries this has lasted,
And we live and keep on guessing.
No one knows.
Dawn follows night,
But happiness—what?

TANYA KUCHERENKO
Age 15

THE EXAM

The exam
Like a clamp
Clutched at her heart.
She waited
And waited
For it to start—
To pass the exam
So that her terror
Would depart.

ANONYMOUS (girl)
Age 9

A SCHOOLBOY'S LAMENT

The days grow ever shorter,
Birds dart past the window,
         having fun,
While I am a prisoner learning
The wretched particles *non* and *un*.

ANONYMOUS (boy)
Age 11

SMALL CHANGE

Thirty kopecks were missing.
A mere thirty kopecks were missing.
Who knows how they disappeared,
Those worn few copper coins.
But they didn't dare to look,
No, they didn't dare to look
Into one another's eyes all evening,
The classroom of students.
Of what importance are thirty kopecks?
A mere miserable thirty kopecks.
No one will remember them
Once that evening has passed.
But it is simply hard for me not to trust,
It is simply hard for me not to trust,
To look forever with suspicion
Upon those who surround me.
School was over late that evening,
I was returning home late that evening.
I felt tired and rotten
Despite all the reasoning,
As from the sky the stars looked down,
As mockingly the stars looked down,
Resembling that evening
Tarnished copper coins.

TATIANA OSTROVSKAYA
Age 15

PERFECTION

It is enough for spring to be itself.
Spring needs no exclusiveness of beauty
       to astound,
As when from the forest foliage in profusion
It sprays dewdrops all around.

But winter—that's another thing:
Its beauty must be strange and stark.
It cannot cast handfuls of color
At flower, bush, and bark.

It is devoid of May's flamboyance,
It is mute, barren, bare.
Winter needs for adornment something other
Than sleeping houses and their icicle stare.

To give it singular perfection,
It has its color of tranquillity,
The passerby looks back and marvels
At its finite stillness, and purity.

GRIGORY OST'OR
Age 13

THE SHORE OF THE UNIVERSE

We are destined
Space maps to chart.
The moment enters history:
Count down: We start!

The far-flung Sea of Dreams
We know we shall reach,
Commune with the universe,
And eternity breach.

No Icarus ever foresaw, not even
In his flights of greatest exaltation,
That Man would make Mother Earth
The launching shore for all creation.

KOLYA ZINOVIEV
Age 14

MY GIFT

Will you take my gift to you
Of the timid murmur of autumn leaves?
And the splendor of sunrise,
And the mystery of evening shadows?

And the saline lips of seas,
The tocsin beat of the last storms?
My peers, will you take my gift to you
Of the Milky Way of early reveries?

Come with me, my friends,
To hear the song of mountain waterfalls,
And the playful pelting of the rains,
And the lure of distant, quiet moorings.

Come, let us build cities in the wilderness,
Let us be the reckoners of stars.
And like Danko,* with our hearts
We shall brave battle warnings and darkness.

Come, let us seed the earth with dreams,
Spread happiness amongst all.
Let there resound over our world
Songs of joy, sounds of laughter.

NATASHA BUKHTEYEVA
Age 15

* A folktale hero who gave his heart to save his people.

Let there always be a sky,
Let there always be a sun,
Let there always be a Mama,
Let there always be a me.

KOSTYA BARANNIKOV

Age 4

SOURCES AND ACKNOWLEDGMENTS

The love of poetry among the young in the Soviet Union is extraordinarily widespread, and the practice of writing poetry is pursued by all, from "that special tribe of versifiers," as the late Kornei Chukovsky admiringly referred to preschoolers, to teen-age schoolchildren. The sources for collecting and selecting from such voluminous creativity are therefore plentiful. Nearly every school, children's library, Palace of Pioneers, and rural, professional or trade union House of Culture has its literary circle for children and young people. Numerous such circles particularly further the writing of poetry, under the guidance of professional teachers or poets eager to advance literary creativity among the young.

The objectives of this extracurricular program, nurtured and administered by the Institute for Esthetic Education of the Academy of Pedagogical Sciences, are thus defined: the "teacher–enthusiast" leading such clubs seeks to encourage literary creativity of schoolchildren in order to help develop their esthetic sensitivity to the written word. Esthetic perceptiveness will further the child's mental and emotional maturity. A relevant purpose is to make the young person into a "talented reader." Through his contact with literature, especially with poetry, and through his own efforts in writing poetry, the child learns to appreciate artistic literature, gaining insights into its esthetic and civilizing elements. The motto has been: "the talented writer needs talented readers." In the process of becoming perceptive readers, the young lovers and composers of poetry at times express themselves with outstanding skill. The fruits of their poetic labors are devotedly gathered.

Collections of children's poems are published in book form. Leading juvenile magazines assign a section to young people's poems. The works of winning participants in poetry contests are broadcast over television and radio. Schools preserve the creative writings of their pupils. Poetry circles collect the work of their members in files of albums. I have drawn from all of these sources for the selections in the present volume.

I have also been assisted by educators and editors and by a number of youthful poets themselves in acquiring unpublished poems, adding them to the several hundred works from which the present selection was made. I am deeply thankful to all of them. But very special gratitude is due to three kind and dedicated people without whose interest the success of my quest would have been limited:

I owe a great deal to the late Kornei Chukovsky, author of *From Two to Five*, in which he revealed the natural love affair between preschoolers and poetry and publicized their verses. The preschoolers' poems in the present collection come mainly from his work.

I am immeasurably in debt for personal guidance and inspiration to Vladimir Glotser, for twelve consecutive years a gifted and dedicated leader of children's and adolescents' poetry circles, author of the remarkable book *Deti pishut stikhi* ("Children Write Verse"), which discusses the schoolchild's poetic creativity with the same perceptiveness and enthusiasm with which Chukovsky writes about preschoolers, and editor of two published collections of poems by members of his circles.

To Vera Kudriashova, for thirty years the leader of children's poetry circles at the Palace of Pioneers in Moscow and editor of publications of young people's poetry, I am most indebted for assistance in making available to me the work of young people under her guidance.

Quite a number of the poems selected for the present collection were given to me directly by the young poets themselves, copied by hand into a "tetrad," a small classroom notebook—all treasured gifts.

Lastly, I want to thank every one of the young people who composed the ninety-two poems I have selected for the privilege of having, and delighting in, their early efforts. Even the strenuous task of translation held a special kind of enjoyment, a unique by-product of the pleasures of poetry.

M.M.

ABOUT THE AUTHOR

MIRIAM MORTON was born in Russia and immigrated to the United States in her adolescence. A graduate of New York University, she has been a social worker and teacher of young children. In more recent years she has become widely known as author, anthologist, and translator, especially of works for and about children. Among her award-winning books are *A Harvest of Russian Children's Literature*, *From Two to Five* by Kornei Chukovsky, and *Fierce and Gentle Warriors*, stories by Mikhail Sholokhov. She has also published notable translations for young readers of stories by Leo Tolstoy and Chekhov, as well as by major French writers. She is the author of *The Arts and the Soviet Child* and *Pleasures and Palaces*.

ABOUT THE ARTIST

EROS KEITH was born in Colorado and attended the University of Chicago and the Chicago Art Institute. Mr. Keith has illustrated many books for children, including *Undine*, which won a 1971 Lewis Carroll Shelf Award, and *Rrra-ah* and *Bedita's Bad Day*, which he also wrote. He lives in New York City.